SO
FAR
SO
BAD

by
Paul Birtill

Hearing Eye

Published by Hearing Eye, Box 1, 99 Torriano Avenue,
London NW5 2RX

ISBN: 1 870841 67 0

This publication has been made possible with the financial
assistance of the London Arts Board.

Printed by Aldgate Press, London E1
Typeset by Daniel James at mondo designo

Some of these poems appeared in the
following publications:

The Guardian, The Express, The Echo Room,
Psychopoetica, Shrike, Rising, Out From Beneath
The Boot

and were broadcast on Radio 100 Amsterdam.

With thanks to Martyn Watts.

CONTENTS

WINTER OF '63

It snows for the first
time. My sister buys a trunk
for college and my father
gives her a black eye as
a leaving present – the
life experience has begun...

SECTIONED

They stand around me in
a big circle – arms folded
faces expressionless. I try
to explain that I'm not mad
and it's all a big mistake.
I plead my case strongly –
passionately as if my life
depended on it; and just
when I think I've won them
over – convinced them I'm
sane – this big black guy
appears from nowhere and
jabs me in the bum with a needle...

DEATH ON THE ROADS

I hate it when death
passes me by suddenly
in the shape of a red
transit van. A few seconds
later and I may have been
tossed into the air – waking
to the voice of a policeman
asking the crowd of morbid
onlookers did they see
what happened...

WHEN DID YOU LAST SEE YOUR FATHER?

Where's your father Paul?
down south miss
What's he doing there?
teaching miss
Why doesn't he teach
up here?
He likes the climate miss
When's he coming back?
Don't know miss
Why isn't he with
his family?
He can't stand us miss
Is that why you shake
your head?
Don't know miss
Alright sit down.

THE ROCK SHOP

We were always making
fun at the man in the
Rock shop. Once he got
very angry and began
throwing his stock at
us – rare stones of
varying colours whizzed
past our ears and my friend
was hit in the face with a
piece of malachite. The police
took him away and his shop
closed down. Some weeks later
he killed himself by swallowing
some pulverised granite.

CHEST PAINS AT 3AM

There goes another speeding ambulance
without its siren on – a heart attack
case – they don't like to cause them
undue stress. But they cause me stress.
I imagine the poor sod lying on a settee
gasping for breath and chewing an aspirin
his frantic wife and kids looking on –
how much easier to die on your own.
I wonder when it will be my turn,
and ring an ambulance to see how
long it takes to arrive – they are
not amused...

MILLENNIUM

It's weird seeing '2000' on things
because I, like some other people,
think the world's going to end –
computers going down, plane crashes...
I wouldn't mind, actually
I'll be forty, and I've got my book out
but my nephew's gutted –
he'll only be sixteen
and he wants a football career...

SIMPLY EVERYONE'S STOPPING
SMOKING CIGARETTES

The butcher's stopped
The dentist's cut down
The priest's switched
to charoots
The fishmonger's on
a pipe and the chemist
is taking snuff – simply
everyone's stopping smoking cigarettes
since the doctor had a heart attack...

WASTE OF TIME

First of all
you search for one.
Then you find you
like them but don't
fancy them.
You fancy them
but don't like them.
You fancy and like
them but they only
like you..
You fancy and like
them but they only
fancy you.·You fancy and like
them and they fancy
and like you – you
both fall in love
and in one to five
years one of you
fancies someone else
and it all ends sour...

SIX O'CLOCK

You make me feel like
a sick pervert – a disturbed
sadist, every time you leave
the room when I turn on the
news, because you don't watch
it and it's so bad...

TEACHERS ARE OVERPAID

Third-rate psychologists
substandard encyclopaedias
second-class citizens
grossly overpaid...

Verbal bullies
too cowardly for the police
talentless, unoriginal –
certificates to prove it. Societies' outcasts
forced back to school...

Unenthusiastic, uninspiring
crashing bores with
a mental problem
so uninteresting as to
need a weapon.
Keep this poison
away from children...

Frustrated failures
enemies of the individual
punishers of creative thought
character assassins
receiving more than road sweepers...

Congenital idiots
award the most unworthy
penalise that which
they don't understand.
Is it any wonder they
occasionally get a kicking?

ON LOSING A MOTHER AT SIXTEEN

A bad age to lose a mother say some
psychologists – neither a boy nor
a man – a mere fledgling leaving
the nest. I was devastated – felt
lost, deserted even betrayed and
found it difficult to relate to
women for a long time after. I
wondered how I would fill all the
years of a life without her; although
as with my father's death some years
later it did give me a new sense of
freedom which I felt slightly guilty
about, but I don't think I could have
lazed around on the dole had she lived.
Like many immigrants she was obsessed
with her children's education and
sadly lived just long enough to learn
I'd failed most of my 'O' Levels.

STRANGLED BY A NEIGHBOUR

No chance to go dancing
No chance to go courting
No chance to have children
Oh to be slain at nine...

No chance to go travelling
No chance to go boozing
No chance to choose careers
Oh to be slain at nine...

No chance to have memories
No chance to have achievements
No chance to make friendships
Oh to be slain at nine...

No chance to grow older
No chance to grow wiser
No chance to be contented
Oh to be slain at nine...

FINAL RESULTS

ABRAHAMS   63 - Bowel Cancer

BAYLISS   48 - Motor Neurone disease

BIRTILL   55 - Heart attack

BYRNE   40 - Suicide

CAMPBELL   86 - Cancer of the stomach

CREWDSEN   66 - Killed on a pedestrian crossing

DODD   29 - Heart attack

DUNCAN   68 - Lung cancer

EARWAKER   71 - Peritonitis

FITZGERALD 38 - Car crash

GILLIN   89 - Old age

HEATH   64 - Lung cancer

HERON   39 - Brain Haemorrhage

JOHNSON   93 - Old age

KENNY   19 - Murdered

KINSELLA   35 - AIDS

LARGE   60 - Heart attack

LEE   42 - Chokes to death

LYNESS B   67 - Leukaemia

LYNESS J   81 - Stroke

MARRAY   73 - Heart attack

MURRY   43 - Brain Tumour

McQUAID   79 - Electrocuted

RASMUSSEN 71 - Heart attack

RYAN   74 - Fractured skull from fall

THOMAS A   87 - Killed in a fire

THOMAS F   60 - Heart attack

TRAYNOR   65 - Stroke

TURTLE   58 - High blood pressure

VENTREE   74 - Heart attack

WEDGWOOD 80 - Cancer of the throat

WELSH   70 - Cancer of the prostate

Good riddance to bad rubbish...

HAVING YOUR PHOTOGRAPH
TAKEN IN LONDON

When someone produces a camera
and takes a photograph in a
London public place I normally
look annoyed and turn away
hoping they'll think I'm a
terrorist, undiscovered
murderer or prisoner on the
run. I have never smashed a
camera though, I wouldn't
take the role that far...

ENGAGED

The operator
has checked the line
and tells me there's
an interesting conversation
in progress.
I didn't think he had
it in him...

ONSET OF MADNESS

One day my sister
quite suddenly, without warning
went mad.
I remember I was in the garden
at the time playing with a friend
when I heard this awful scream.
I thought someone had had an
accident and froze. But then
came the sound of laughter
followed by more screams
and then shouting from my father.
'What's happening in there' asked
my friend I said I didn't know.
Then suddenly the kitchen door
flung open and my sister ran into
the garden naked screaming at the
top of her voice with my father
chasing after her. He told me to
dial 999 and ask for an ambulance,
my friend left...

PUB COLLECTION

They came round
again tonight with
their death-defying tins
collecting for bee-stings
to the throat violent
murder falling off
mountains getting
struck by lightning
fires and gas explosions
and I said:

"You can die of cancer too"...

TO NO LONGER BE ME

I don't want to lose me
I've grown used to me,
me is all I know.
I don't wish to lose
all my knowledge, memories
experiences, even my neurosis.
I know of no other existence
except being me. I can handle
saying good-bye to others,
but not me – we've shared so much...

CRUEL TO BE KIND

There was a man
who lived on his own
who behaved in a way
that no one should
ever love him – ignored
the game and social graces
and didn't break a single heart...

LIFE GOES ON

I dislike people
because they're
always getting
over things.
With such ease
they carry on
because they say
life must go on
but must it?
and is this really
the case or are they
just insensitive
miserable little
earthlings with
not much feeling
at all...

LOOSE CHANGE

Who would have the loose change
on my sideboard if I died today?
Would it be shared amongst my
family – given to my nephew for
pocket money – or put towards my
funeral expenses? Who would have
the loose change on my sideboard
if I died today?

OH GOD

Human beings are
confused little children
who know nothing about
anything. They don't even
know if they'll wake up
tomorrow and see another day.
They get absorbed in money,
politics and careers of every
sort – all diversions from the
truth – temporary refuge from
the terrible, unpalatable, unavoidable
truth – that they are dying, slowly
but surely each sombre day, hooray!

SO FAR SO BAD

How come I've ended
up like this
lying in my
own piss.
With no partner
or job – a
fifteen stone slob.
Each day as empty
as the last, no
future or present
only the past...

IMAGINE

Imagine if the only
way of dying was to
be kicked to death.
There would be thousands
of kickings every minute.
Every time you went out
to buy a newspaper you'd
see someone being kicked
to death; and you'd always
be wondering just when and
where and by whom you were
going to get your fatal kicking...

BARGAIN

My next door neighbour – strange woman,
smoked eighty Kensitas a day and collected
the coupons feverishly. I've saved enough
to buy a clock she said after having a lung
removed – I've just got a toaster she said
as her right leg came off. Will you collect
my portable television, she asked me as she
lay in hospital having had her third stroke
and a few years later as she lay dying what
seemed to upset her most was that she was
only ten points off a gorgeous mahogany coffin.

I DON'T THINK SO

Was the poem
good enough though?
Was it worth tapping
her on the shoulder
for the third time
to borrow her pen
again?

COUCH POTATO

Bet there's no-one
down the local I know
and the tickets for
that concert are all gone...

Bet that new restaurant's
a bleedin' rip off and that
night class is over-subscribed...

Bet there's a crush at
the football match and
they're not saying much
at that meeting...

Bet I wouldn't click
if I went to that club
and that party's a
false address

May as well just lie here
        and watch TV...

DEVASTATED

Yesterday I spent three
hours making a stew and
then dropped it on the
carpet. I was so upset
I rang the Police they
told me not to be so
stupid and asked me if
I lived on my own.

DEAD ERNEST

Ernest Hemingway
wasn't gay
but blew his brains out
anyway...

THE LEAST POPULAR ART FORM

Seventy per cent of poetry
is utter crap
meaningless nonsense
tedious dung
written by bores with nothing
to say who disguise the fact
in clever word play.
The vast majority of it
is fraudulent wanking and
should be thrown in the dustbin.
One shouldn't waste one's time
even looking at it, never mind
reading it and only a fool with
time on his hands attempts to
decipher it...

DEPRESSION

A great black hollow
which needs no feeding
it has no appetite
which hates the dawn
and longs for night
which needs no company
and gets none either
which does not work
just lies there still.

BIG LET DOWN

When I was a boy I would visit
my local library each Saturday
and borrow books about the lives
of famous people. Then I'd sit
and wonder what great, exciting
adventures lay before me. Now
I'm an old man and as my life
draws to a close I realise it's
all been a big let down. No leading
my armies into battle. No great
speeches in parliament. No Oscars,
Nobel prizes or travelling to exotic
places – not even an illicit love affair.
Just recently I've taken to borrowing
those same books again, but instead of
reading them I take them home and deface them.

PSYCHOLOGICAL GAMES

He doesn't care for monopoly
nor is he interested in chess.
He won't play cards or scrabble
but he does like power games and
will play them if you let him...

ENEMIES

I sometimes wonder what it would
be like to sit in a room full of
all the people who dislike me –
yet don't know each other – would
their common loathing of myself
unite them? Are they similar types
perhaps? Would they all get along?
And would I survive the experience?

LIFE'S NOT SHORT ENOUGH

Imagine if the lifespan
was only twelve – what
nicer people you and me
and how much simpler life
would be.

RESULT!

I've got a new girlfriend
who just happens to be my
doctor, and she wants to
see me again – she said
come back in a month's time.

POEM

Delivering the light of
madness, only to be snatched
away by the changeable
movements of the night – the
forgotten hero the moon watches
curiously and absorbs the chaos
of the moment...

LOST

You were miserable,
you said unhappy because
you were alone, inadequate
with no partner – not a unit.
Yet you painted pictures –
beautiful pictures of beautiful
cats. Now you have a man and are
happy? But paint pictures of tall
buildings and machinery or worse
don't paint at all.

...BASTARDS, NOT YUPPIES

A disease from the Home Counties
with money to spend
ambitious, competitive
striving little bleeders
Out to make good in their chosen fields
making London a shit place to be
Bastards...

High spirits and barbecues
parachute jumps for Cancer Research
Jogging in the Marathon
giving blood after a game of squash
Bastards...

Stinking lovers of life
buying up tree houses
on Hampstead Heath
Happy letters to Mummy and Daddy
admirers of Geldof and Waite
contempt for mining Arthur
Bastards...

Jeffrey Archer on the tube
night classes in French
travelling around Europe
with an old school pal
Independent as fuck
Bastards...

Wonderfully exciting
vibrant personalities
generating warmth and happiness
wherever they are
such fun to be with
when the bubbly flows
Bastards...

Accident! Did you see?
one of them got killed
crossing Baker Street
the other day
around 1:35
Nice one Lord...

POSITIVE THINKING

The muck used to cope with
life's continuous programme
of disasters – a pick-you-
up of self-deceit that grows
more cunning as the calamities
get more desperate.

SOLDIER IN THE SOIL

One summer I helped my dad dig
up the garden and found a beautiful
tall soldier buried in the soil.
It had obviously been there a long
time and none of us could make out
what army he belonged to. So my
father suggested we take it round
to Mister Dargy, an embittered old
army officer from World War One.
He wasn't very happy about being
disturbed but examined the soldier
closely and then roared 'I know who
this fellow is - he's a damned yellow
belly, a conscientious objector' and
bit its head off – I cried all the
way home.

JOE'S CAFE

There's bits of egg on
my liver because he only
uses one frying pan. There
are peas in my beans –
he couldn't care less
his place is a mess.
The fella opposite picks
his nose, the fella behind
coughs and splutters –
everyone stares at each
other's food. The tables
are filthy and there's
a bit of dog-dirt near
the door – think I'll
skip dessert.

HIGH PRICE

I only wanted a shag,
now I'm married with
three kids – working
all the hours God sends
and her mother stays most
weekends – wish I'd had
a wank instead...

MISANTHROPIST

He soon realised there
was no advice to be given
and no-one to respect and
without anything original
to offer became a hermit –
the alternative being a
liar or a cheat.

BEING FAT WITH MY CAT

I don't mind being fat, when I'm at
home with my cat. But when I go out
I always feel stout – people laugh
and people stare, but I don't care,
because I don't mind being fat when
I'm at home with my cat...

THE AGNOSTIC PRAYS

He never makes
the sign of the cross
or gets down on his
hands and knees.
He never prays
to a specialist saint
but he prays all the same,
and sometimes he wonders
whether his unconventional
prayers are ever answered
and by whom.

TWISTED

He was nice to me
when his girlfriend
was horrible to me
and was horrible to
me when his girlfriend
started to like me yet
I didn't like either
but was polite to both...

LONDON BARS

You never meet anyone
in a London bar, anyone
you know that is. London
bars are full of strangers –
lone rangers out on their
own or in pairs of two, they
won't talk to you.

You'll never make friends
in a London bar, even if you
travel far. They're unfriendly
places full of unknown faces
you never meet anyone in a
London bar...

DEATH

Total shutdown
an eternal state
of nothingness
a restless spirit
an awful dream
another life
a burning fire
        I'm scared...

DRAMA SCHOOL

When we're young we
train to be actors
and play all kinds
of roles. When we are
older and leave our
acting is better, even
good and sometimes if
we're lucky we get the
parts we want...

CALL FOR SOCKS AND UNDERPANTS

Socks and underpants
socks and underpants
We need socks and underpants
Men's Hostel Old Kent Road
        ...NO TIME WASTERS...

VIOLENCE AND CELIBACY

Men without women
glare at you in bars
don't wash or shave
sing or smile and
thump you at the
drop of a hat...

C OF E UPBRINGING

God mentioned once
Sunday school twice
lose virginity at ten
rock n' roll in teens
plenty of sex
drugs galore
horoscopes
I-Ching
palm readings
and witchcraft
hippy books
eastern mysticism
existentialist arsehole.
No respect
no guilt
no idea
totally confused –
divorced with kid
called Zoe at 25
and no better than
the wild beasts of
the jungle
C of E upbringing…

NO THANKS

Pendulous melons
and open wounds
that smell of fish
is not my dish…

CHANGES

I'm always wondering where
to move to – where I would
be happiest – city, country,
seaside. But really I would
like to move back to my childhood
to see the sky again for the
first time – the sun the stars
the snow – to climb trees and
run in the long grass. Then it
wouldn't matter where I was
because childhood is beautiful
anywhere…

PIGS AND SEX

Most people are ugly
and there's too much
sex about anyway – so
abstain you ugly fuckers
and leave sex to the good
lookers.

NEIGHBOURS

Neighbours
        lie
Neighbours
        spy
Neighbours
        die
                bye…

I KEEP WANTING TO LOOK
AT THAT MAN'S FAT ARSE

It's big and round
and a fly's just
landed on it.
I can't take my eyes
off that man's fat arse.
It doesn't interest me
in the slightest – not at all
but still I stare and my
girlfriend has noticed.
It's just moved a bit to
the right. I must stop this now…

IF YOU'RE NOT BUYING DON'T TOUCH

Arranged marriages
aren't so bad
one avoids the
selection, elimination
– wine tasting process.
I've been spat out
on several occasions…

FORTUNE TELLER

I don't need you
cried the old man
I'm eighty-four I know what
happened...

NO MORE REPRODUCTION

The first century was an experiment
The second was proof
The last eighteen sheer evil
only a nuclear war will
stop us sick bastards now...

NEGATIVE EXPERIENCE

Death makes every
single thing you
do in life absolutely
pointless...